Trillium

A Photo Essay

by

Stephen M Kraemer

© 2019 Stephen M. Kraemer

On the trail

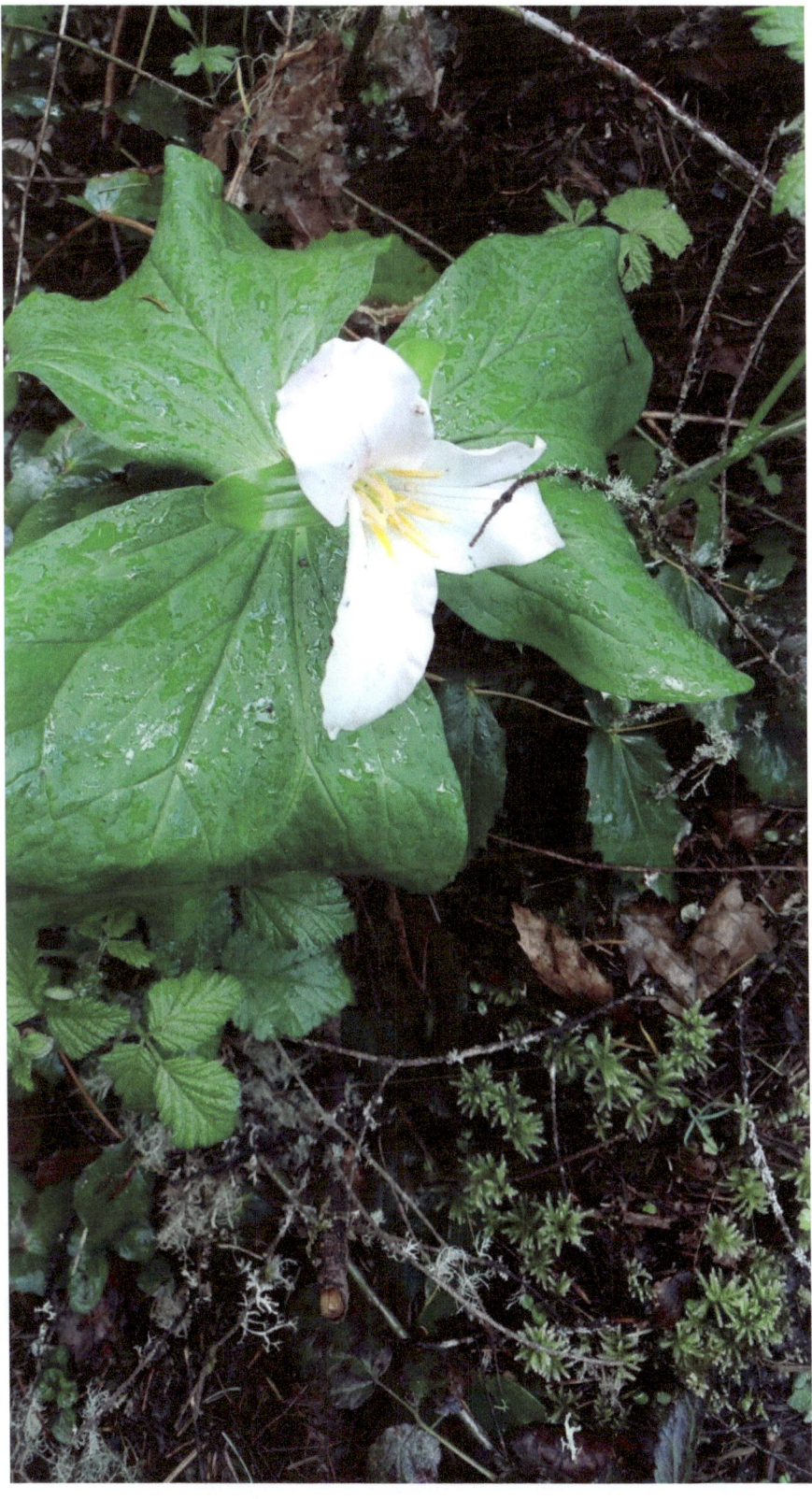

True

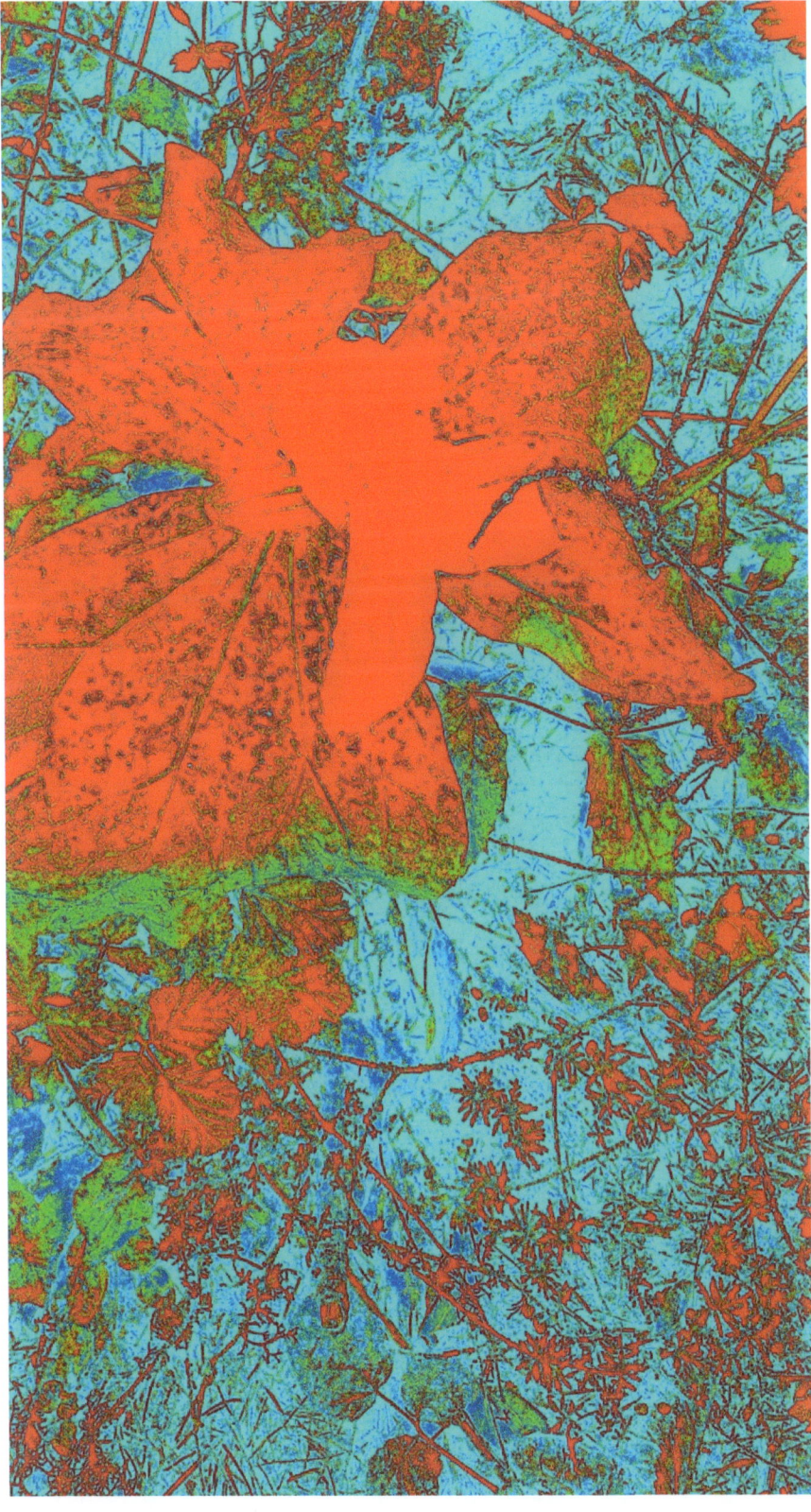

Color

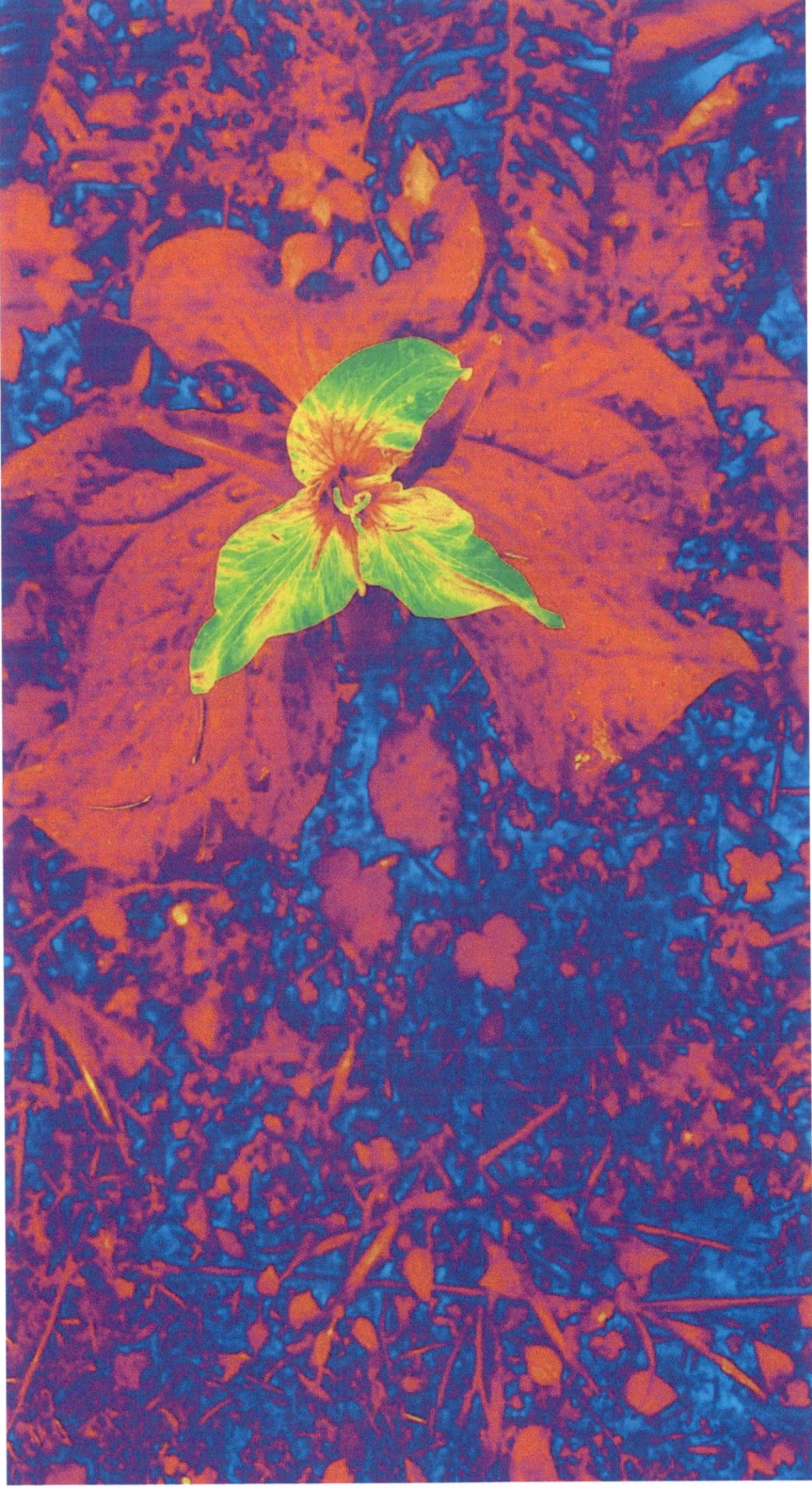

White

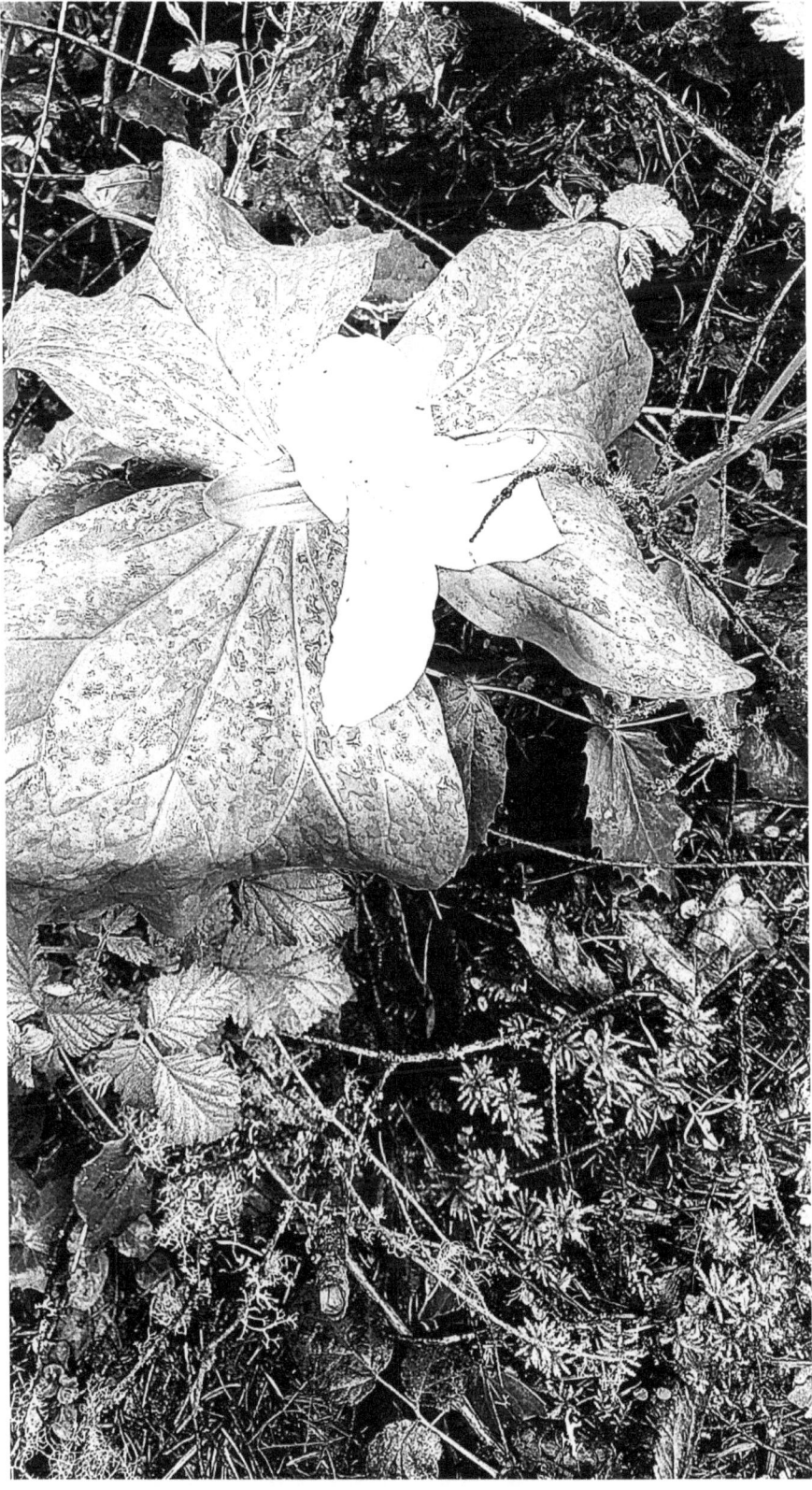

Blend

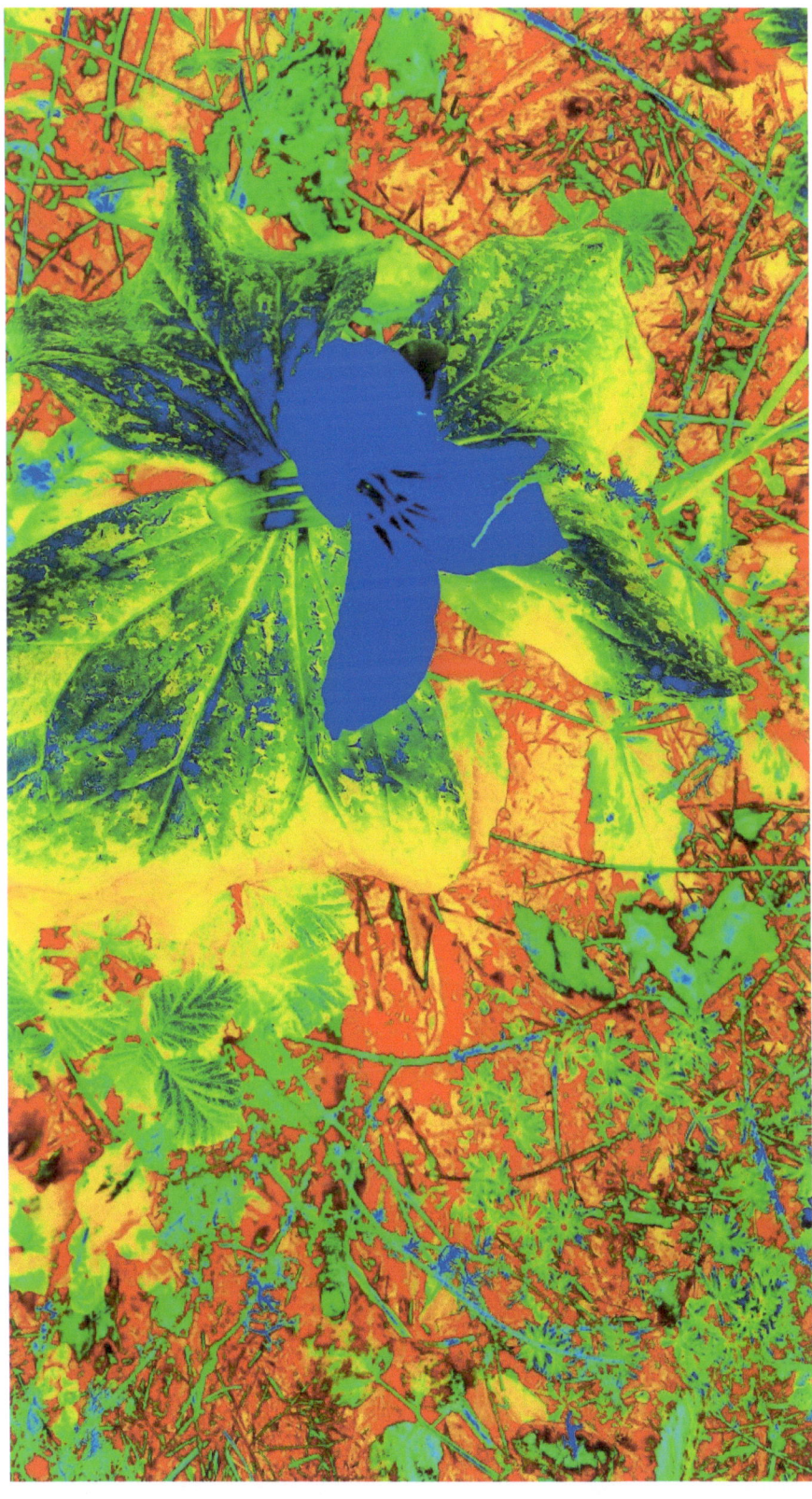

Cool

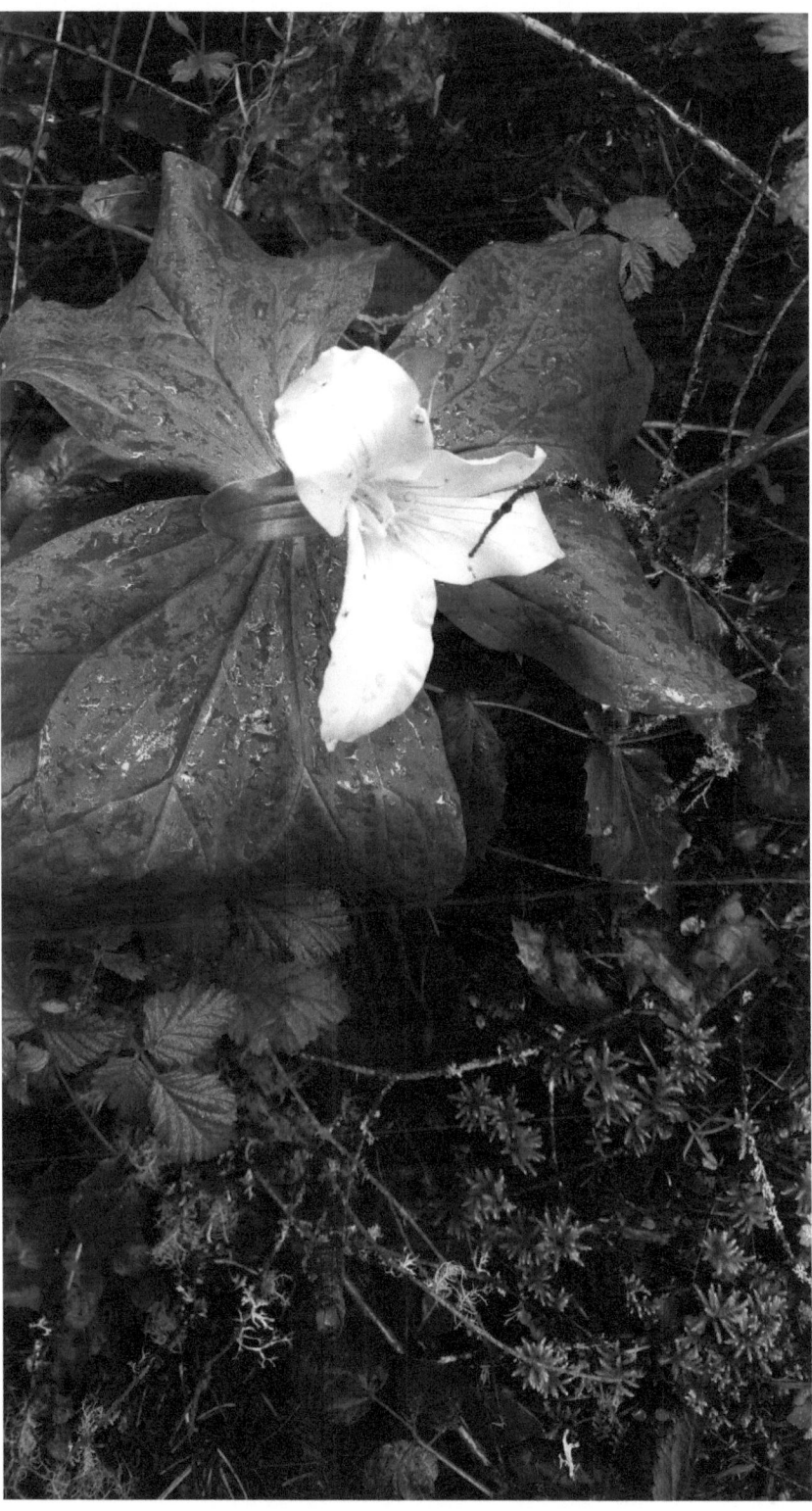

TriColor

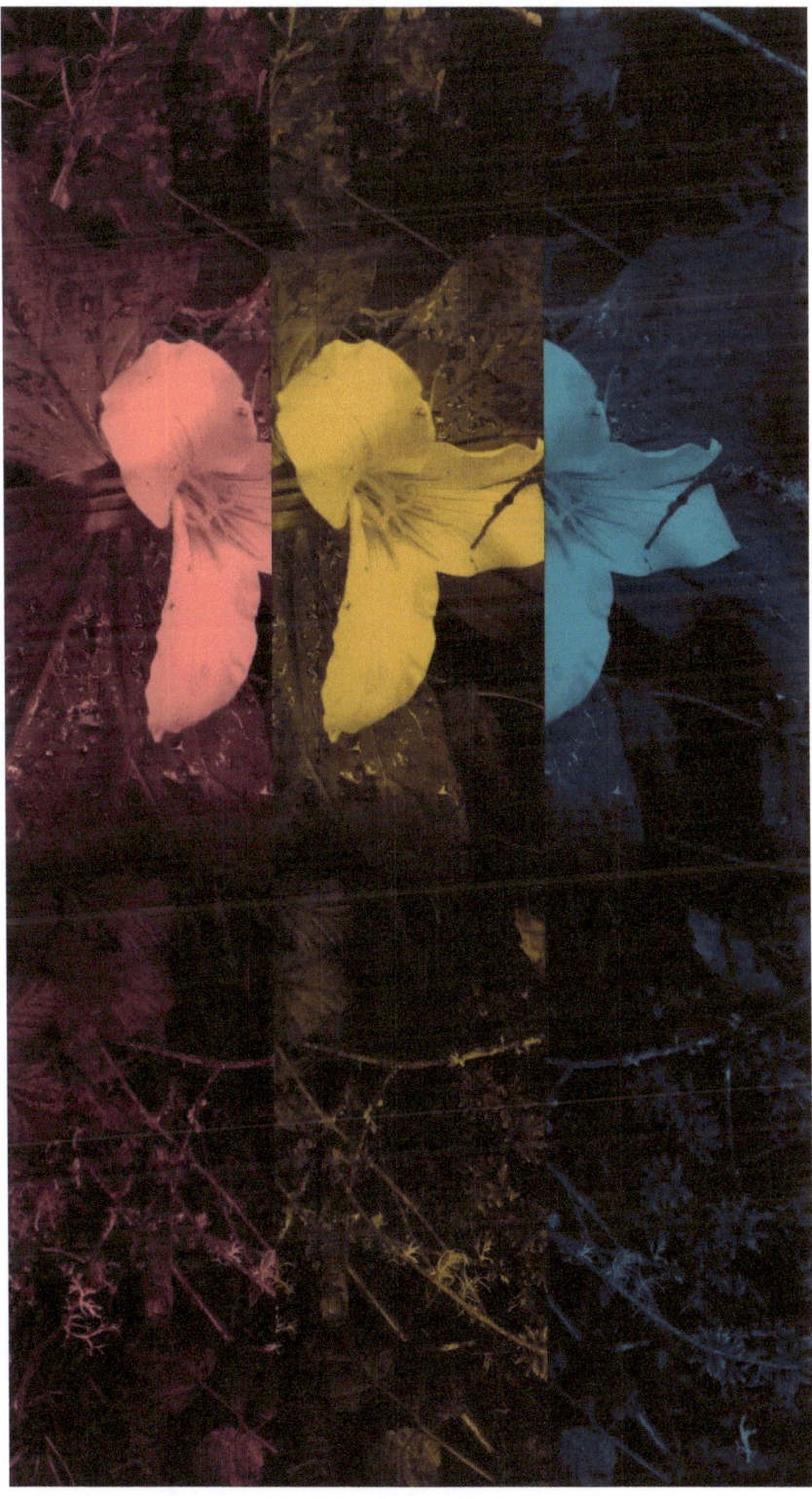

Fall

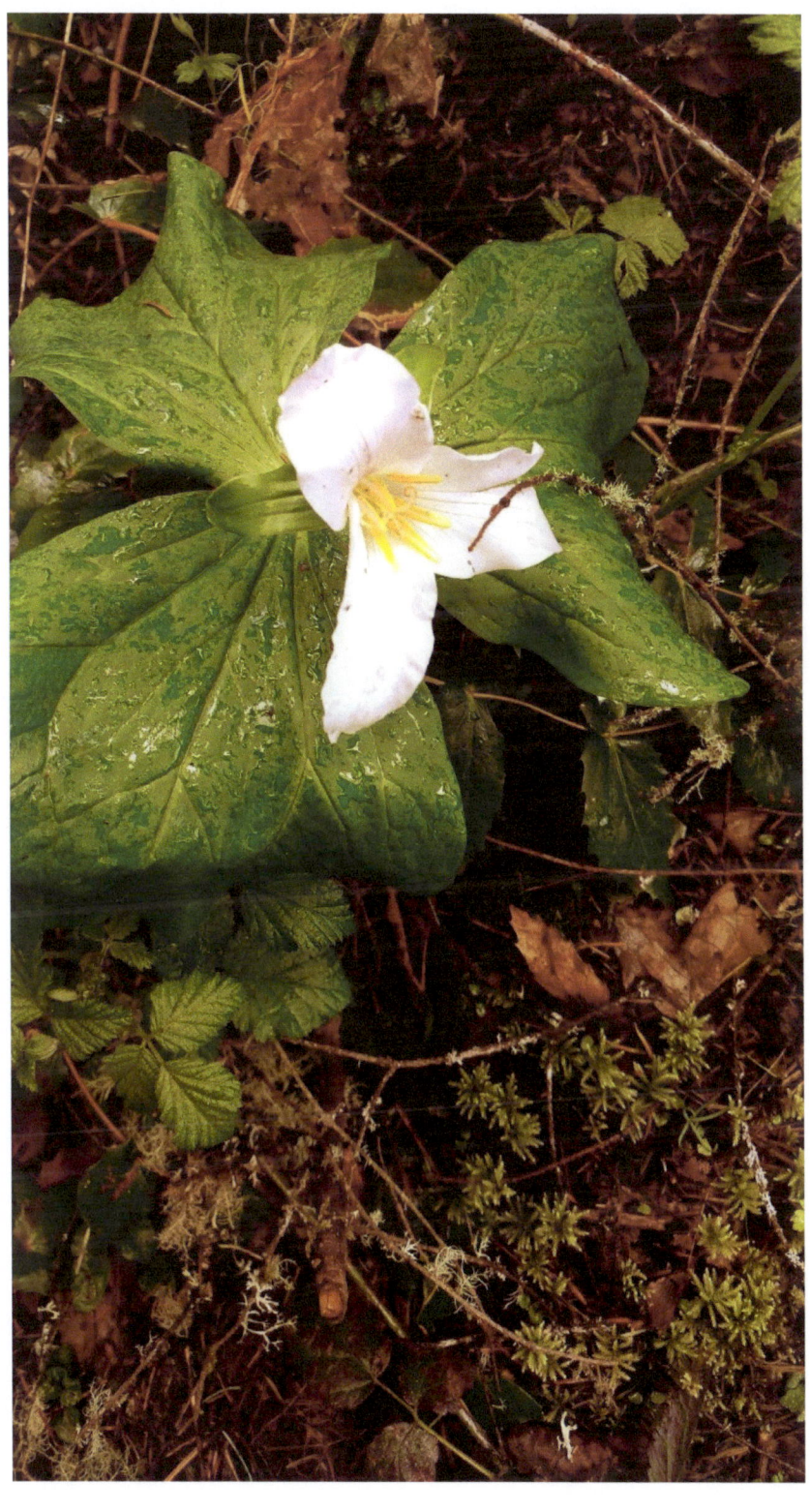

Double

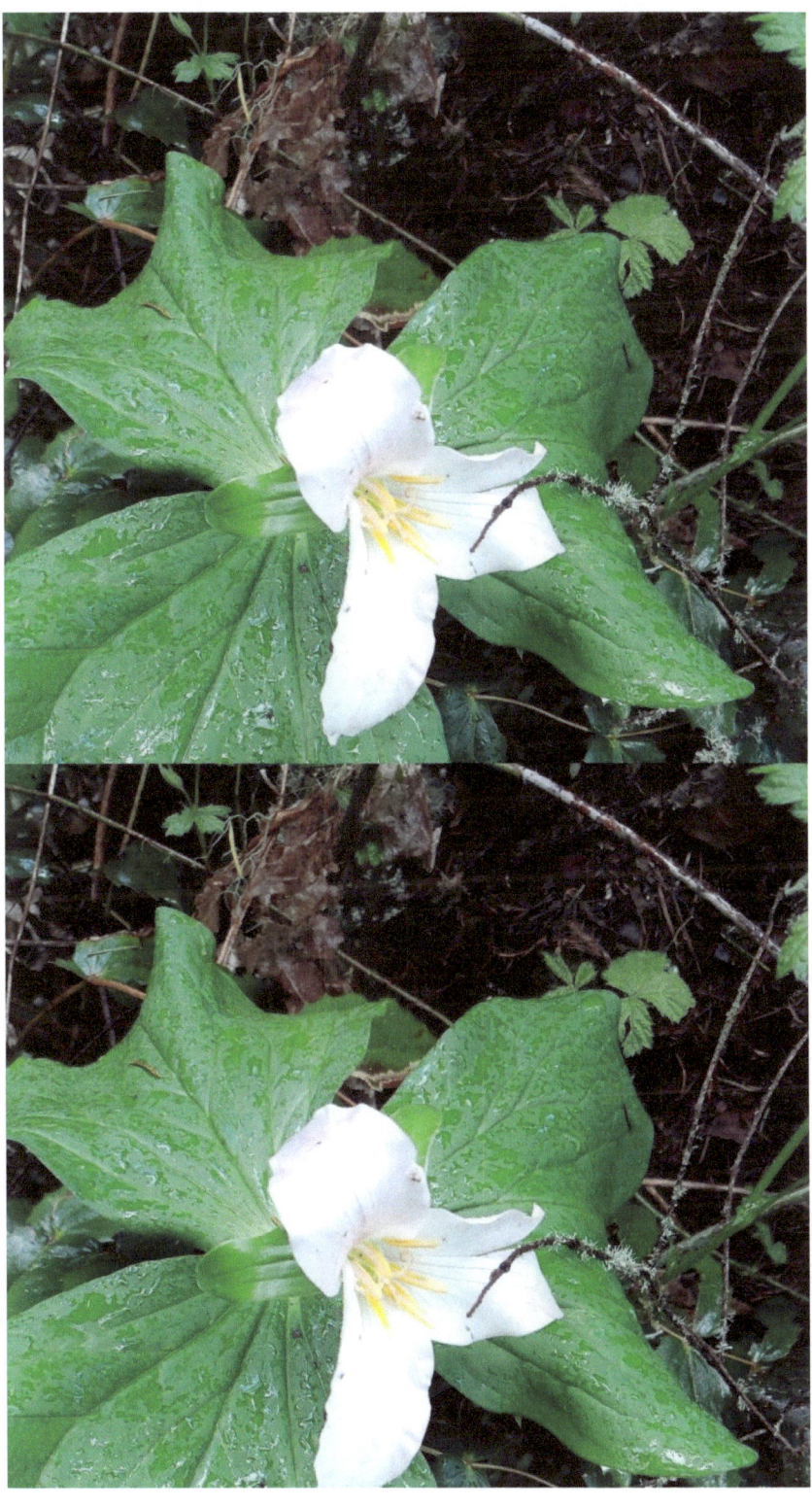

Red

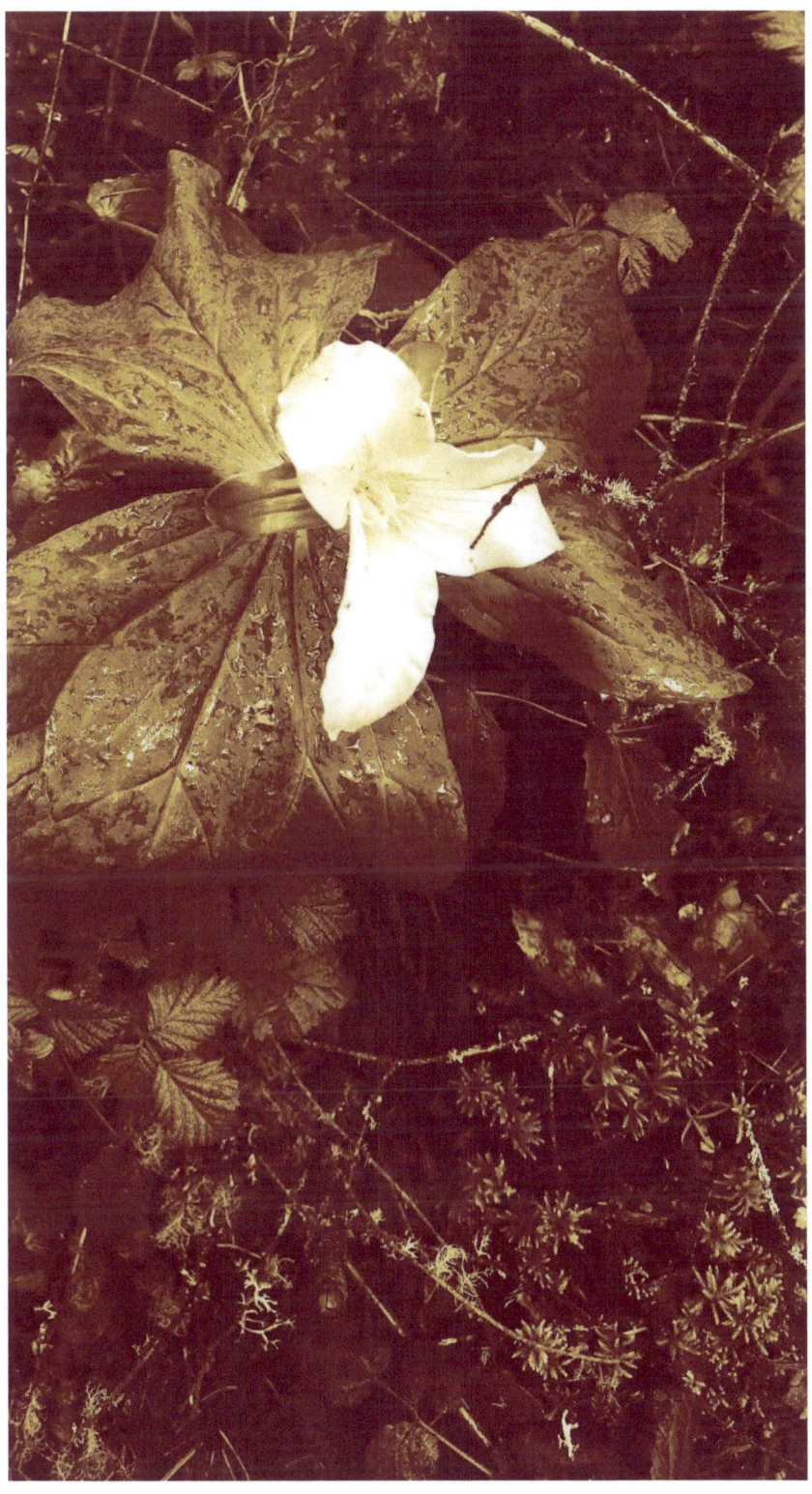

Ice

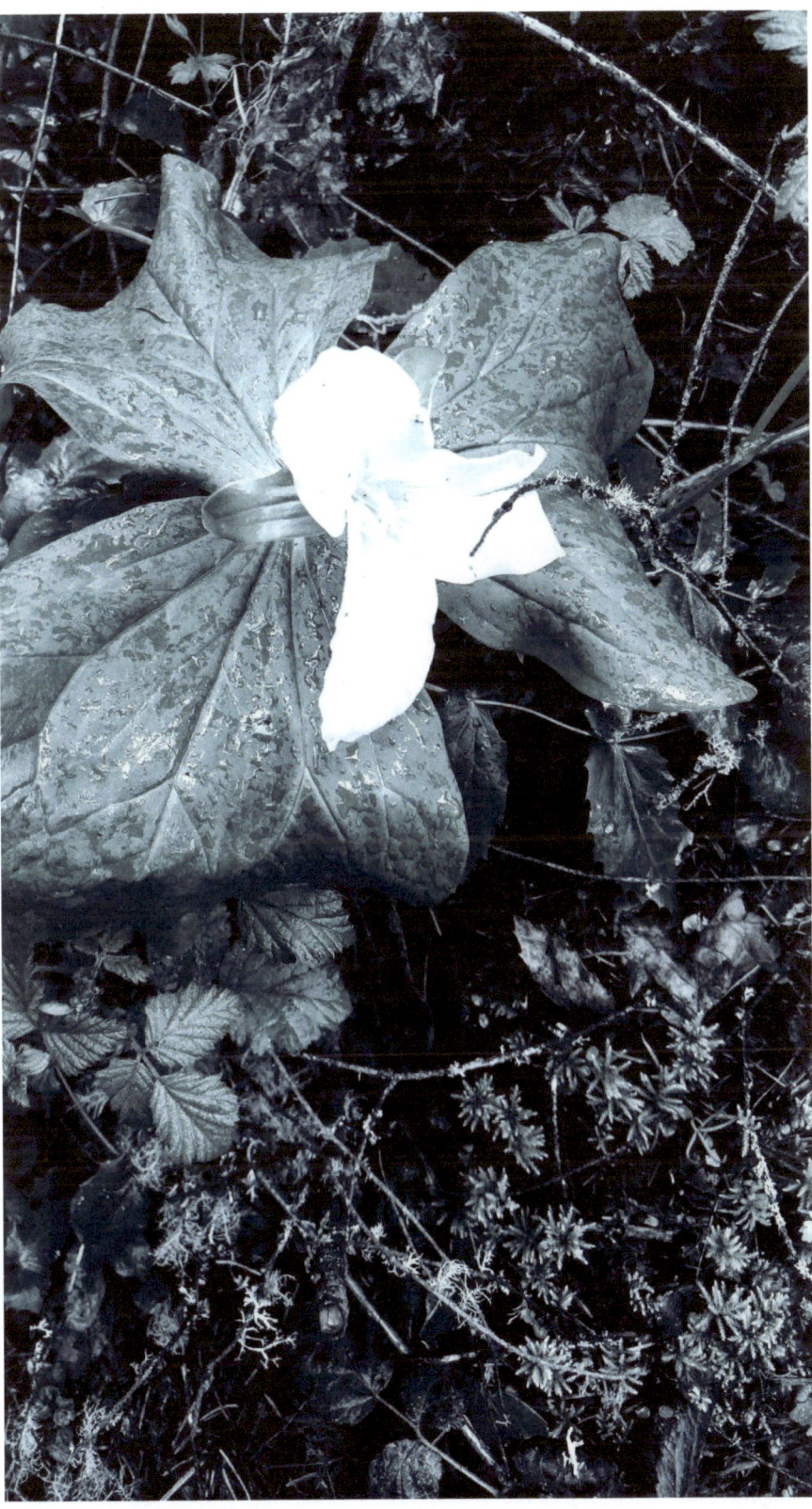

Warm

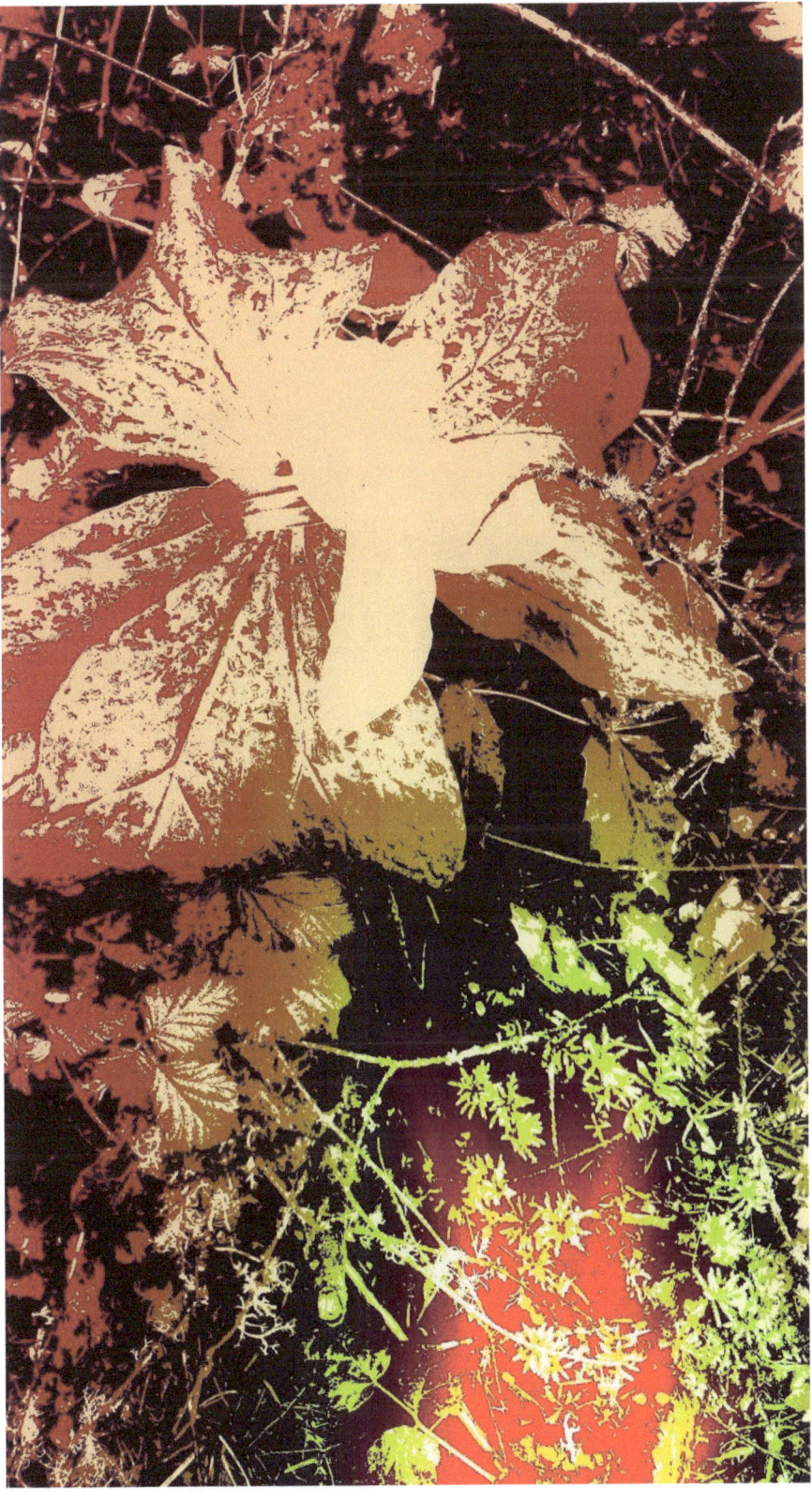

Blue

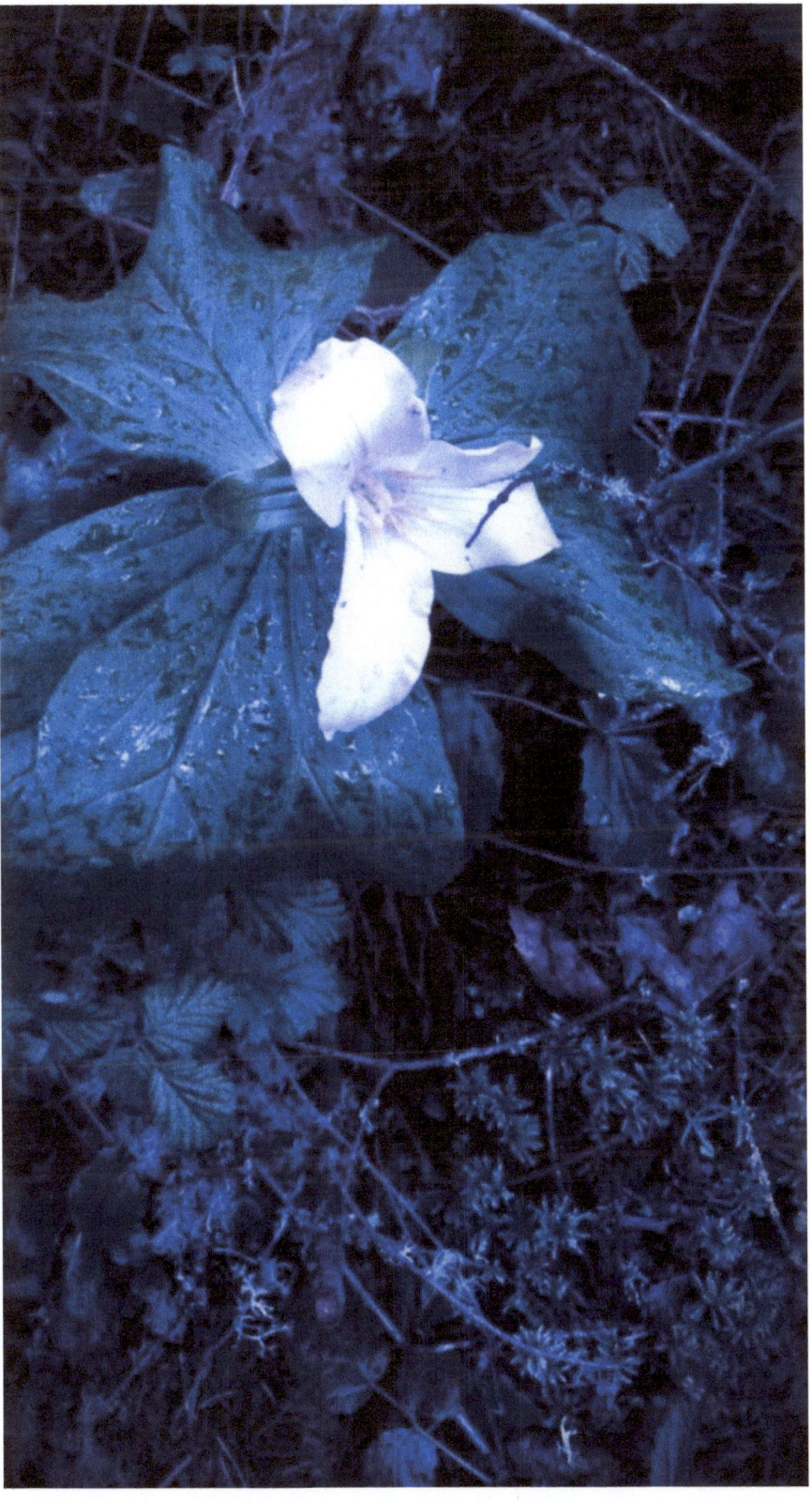

Black

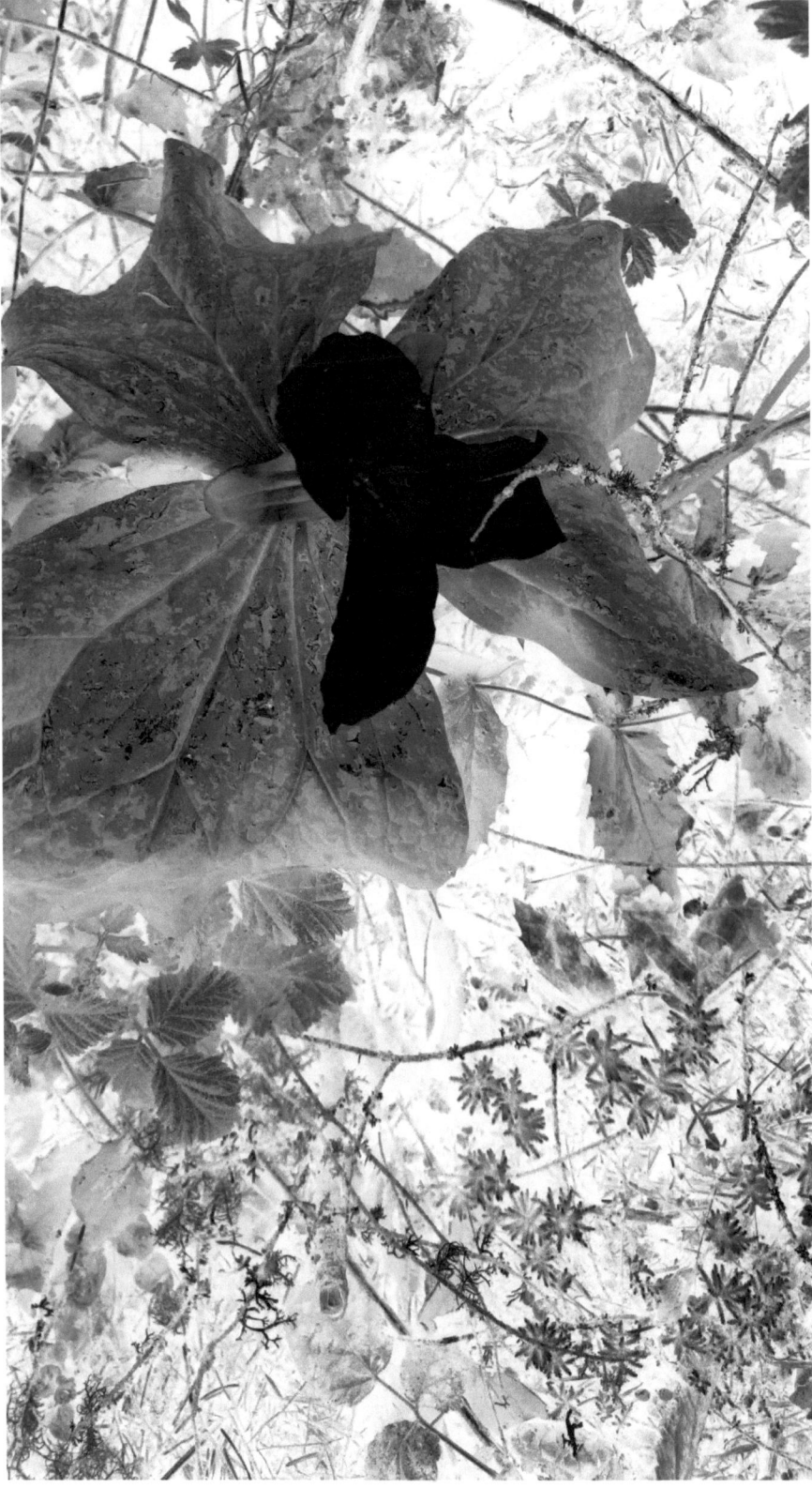

Colors

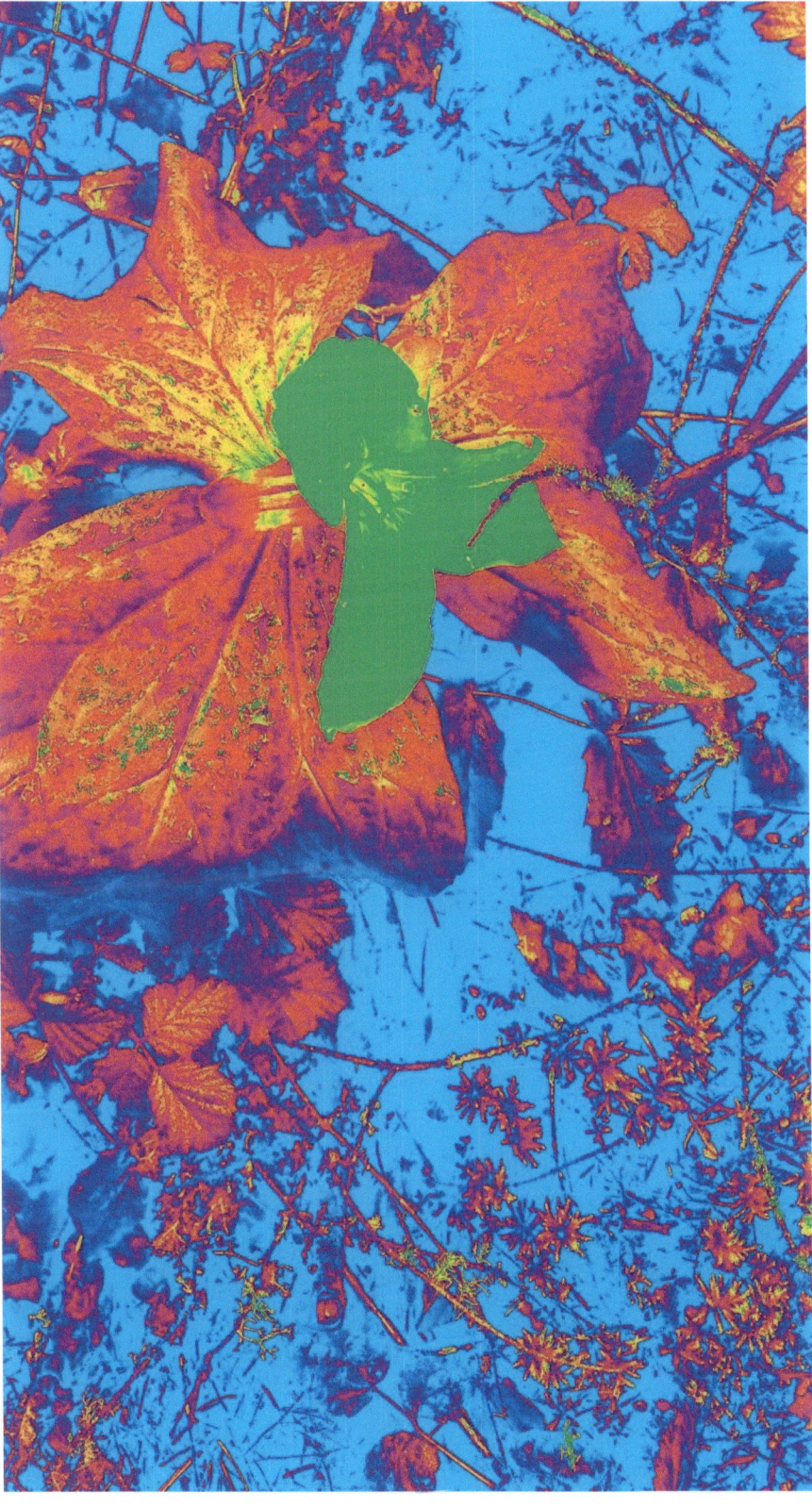

Multiple

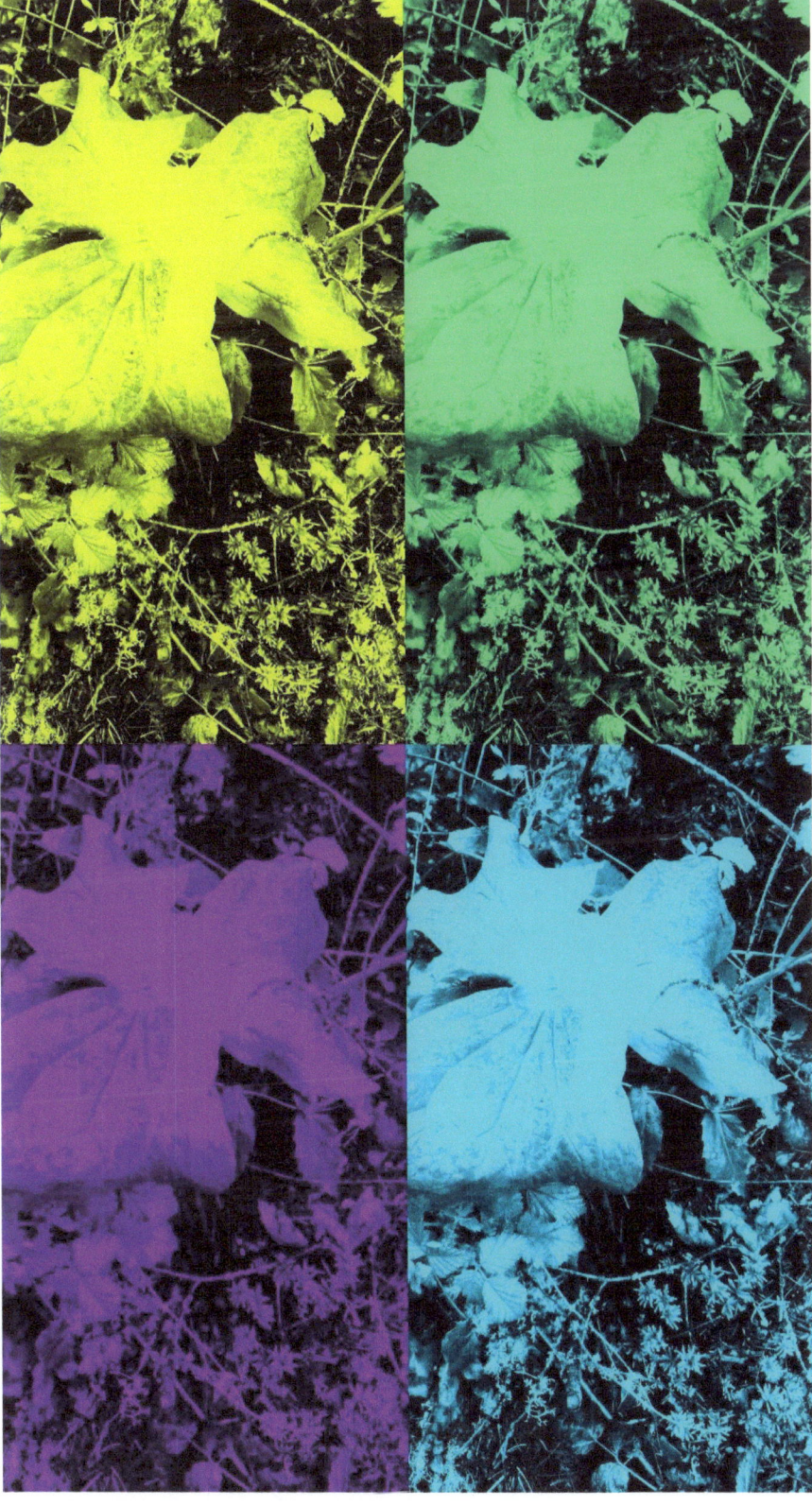

Bright

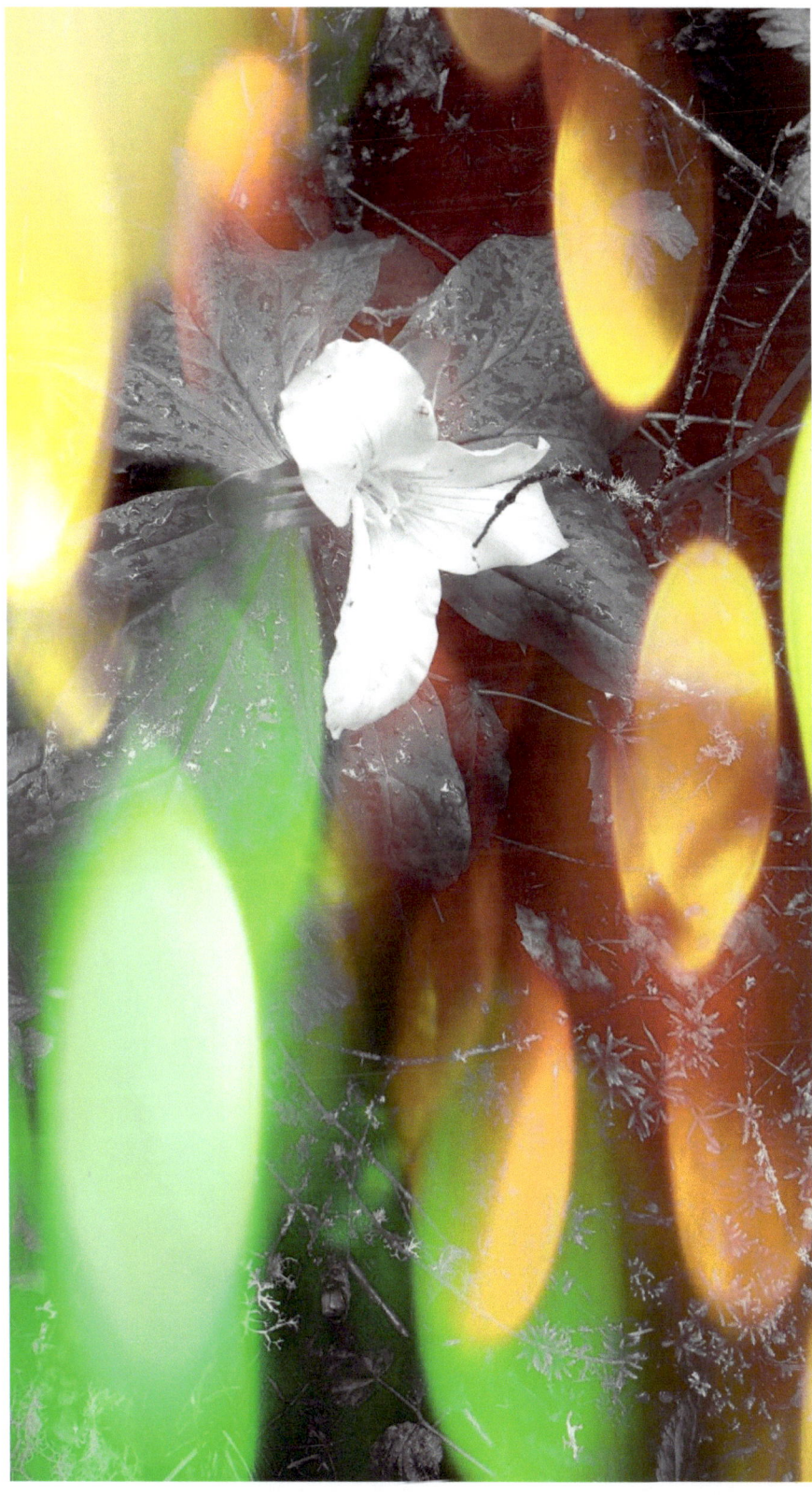

Midnight

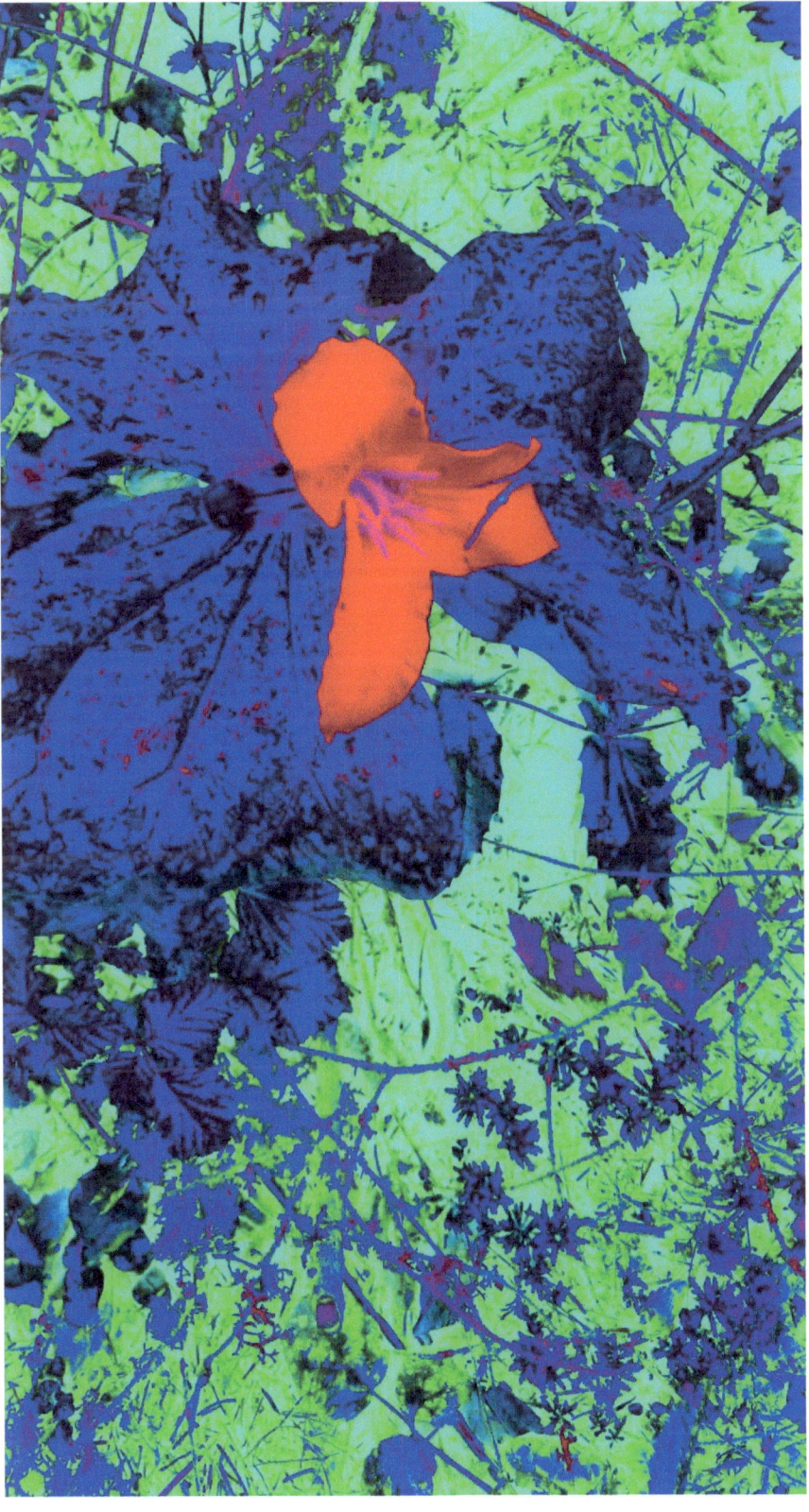

Blossom

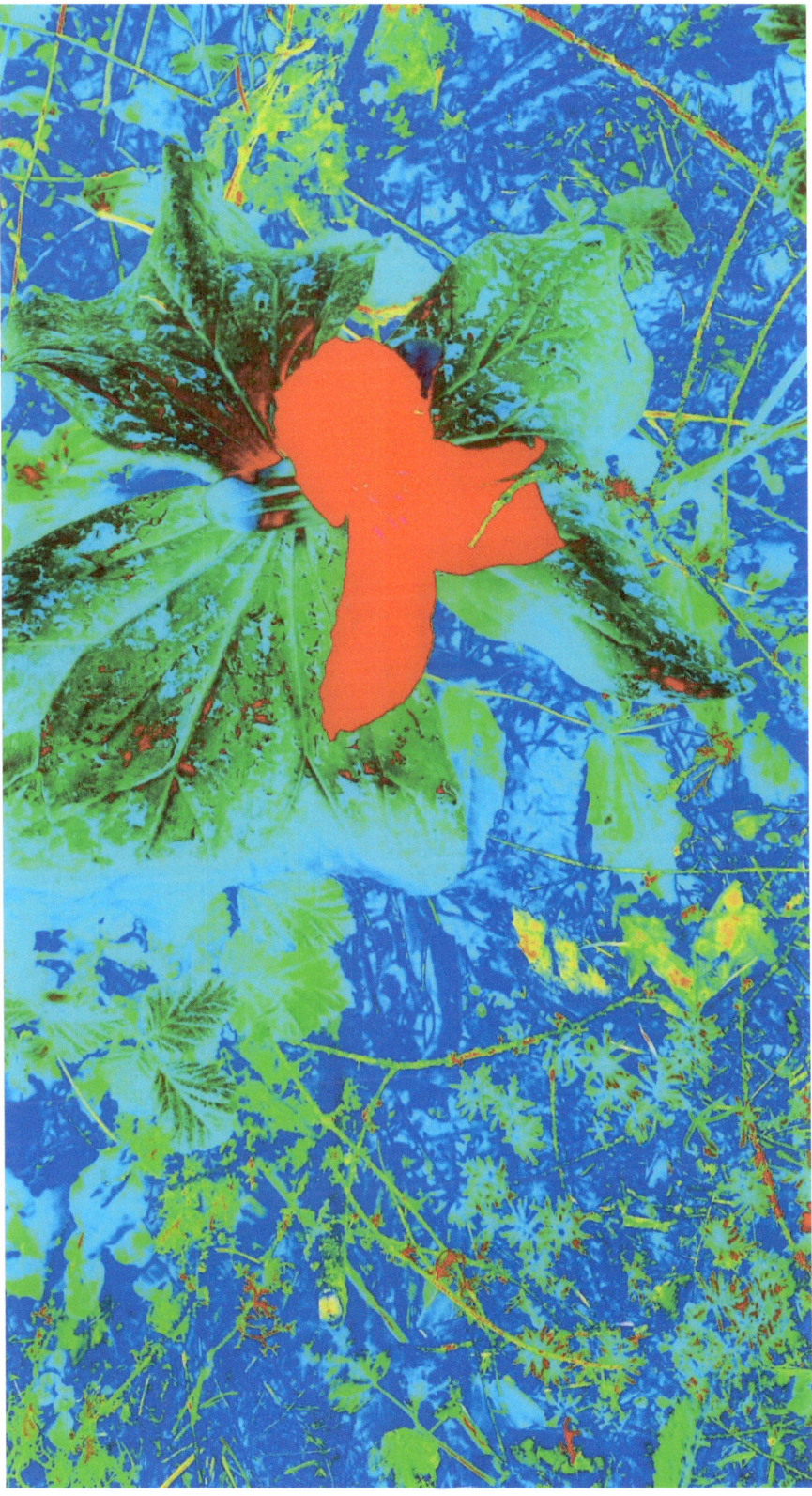

Purple

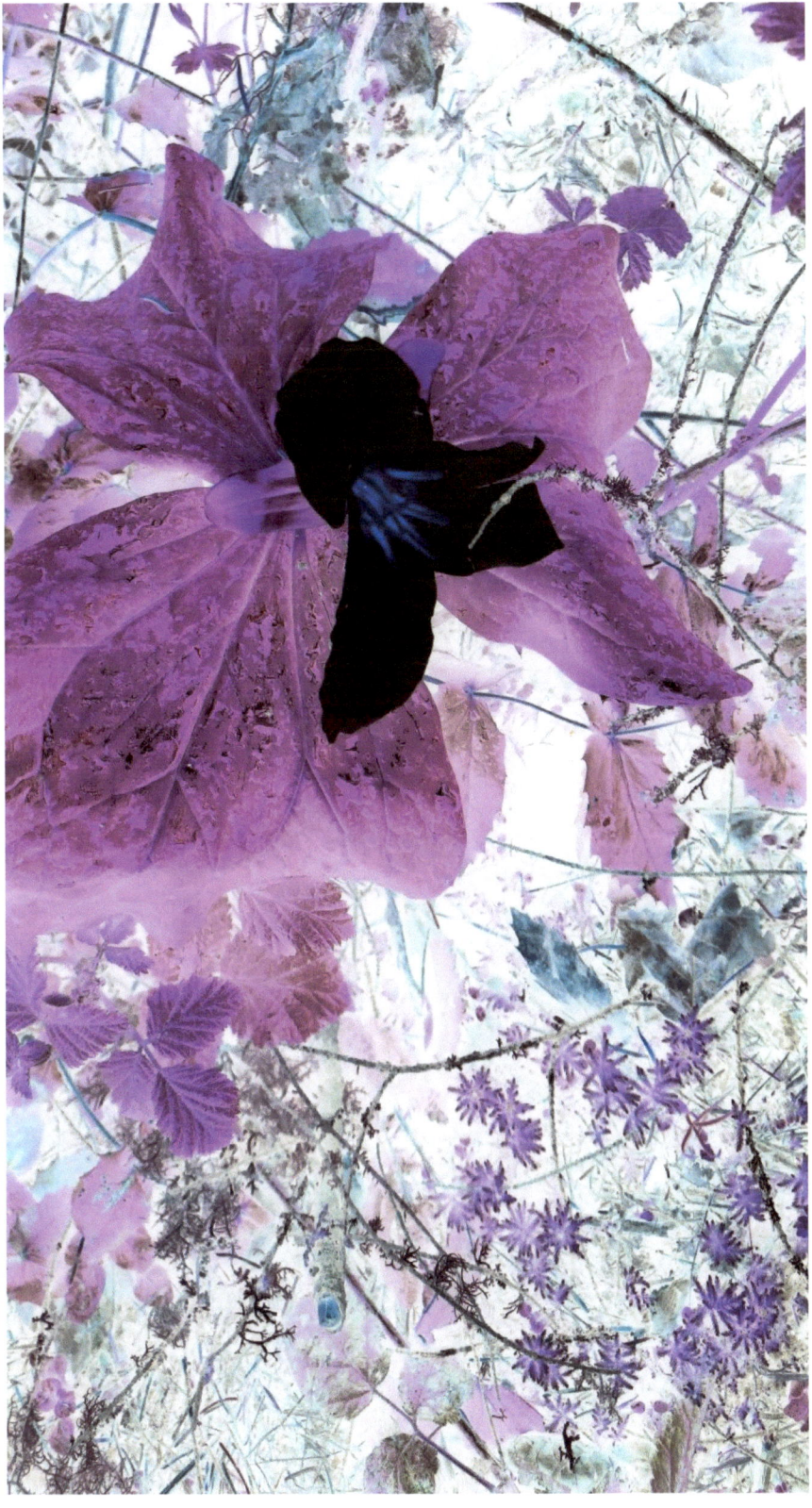

www.ingramcontent.com/pod-product-compliance
Lightning Source LLC
Chambersburg PA
CBHW040251220526

45473CB00001B/449